Lover, Mother & Other

Annika Oakley

BookLeaf Publishing

Presentation by *BookLeaf Publishing*

Web: www.bookleafpub.com

E-mail: info@bookleafpub.com

ISBN: 9789395756709

First edition 2022

DEDICATION

This book is dedicated to Toilet-Duck. Thank you for showing me what a healthy relationship is, and for showing me what love and trust truly look like. I love you. x

ACKNOWLEDGEMENT

Thank you to all those amazing people who were there for me when I needed you most. To Ashlee, Bec, Heather & Jade - thank you for always having the time to listen to me and supporting me unconditionally. Thank you to my parents - Dash & Shane, for all your support. Thank you to my grandparents - Ray & Doreen, for being two of the greatest grandparents I could have ever asked for, I miss you. Thank you to my love - Trent, for helping me heal, supporting my journey, and loving me as I am. And lastly, thank you to my children - I love you so much, and I'm so grateful you chose me to be your mama.

PREFACE

Annika wrote this book mostly for herself, to release those emotions felt in everyday life. This book came from a place of reflection and healing as she travels on her own personal journey of self-love and self-discovery. She hopes you all embark on your own journey of self-love and discovery. She encourages you read to these poems with an open mind and open heart and know that life is a journey, filled with ebs and flows.

She is sunshine.

She is strong.
She is fierce.
She is wild.
She is free.

She is creative.
She is kind.
She is selfless.
She is fair.

She is passion.
She is romance.
She is deep.
She is powerful.

She is worthy.
She is beautiful.
She is sunshine.
She is me.

Take the leap.

Make a change,
If this isn't the life you want for yourself.
If you aren't truly happy,
If you don't feel like the best version of you.

If you want to feel better,
If you want to be better,
If you want to do better,
Make a change.

Be brave,
Be bold.
Take the leap,
Make a change.

It's chemistry.

It's the way he holds me,
Pulling me closer, protecting me from the world.
The way he gently kisses me,
Making me fall deeper and deeper.

It's his hands all over my body,
Appreciative of every curve.
The desire in his eyes,
Relishing in my mind, body and soul.

It's the way he looks deep into my eyes,
Exposing all my nerves.
The intimacy between us,
Like nothing I've ever felt before.

It's our body's intertwined,
Connected on a deeper level.
The passion, love and desire,
Shared between the two of us.

A little bit of love.

Forehead kisses.
Enveloping hugs.
Sharing stories.
Making memories.

Laughter & smiles.
Secret whispers.
Desire & lust.
Wonderful sex.

Adorable nicknames.
Distance apart.
Encouragement.
Trust.

Communication.
Vulnerability.
Intimacy.
Love.

Ocean to the land

She is drawn to him,
Like the ocean to the land.
His presence calms her,
Like a soft breeze on a still day.

He looks deep into her eyes,
A rough sea of heartache.
Her hand in his,
He heals her pain.

Hes drawn to her,
Like the ocean to the land.
Her company leaves him enamoured,
Shes like rain on a summer day.

She looks deep into his eyes,
A calm sea of security.
His hand in hers,
They take the leap.

It's so much happiness.

Moments of passion and intimacy.
Falling slow but fast.
Deep and meaningful.
Not about the destination.
Enjoying the journey.

Deep eye contact.
Laughter and inside jokes.
Comfortable silence.
Light and dark conversation.
Love with acceptance of the past.

Fear of the unknown.
Trust it will work.
Excitement for the future.
Happiness exuding.
Love in its most pure form.

All the feels.

Find a guy that makes you laugh,
Somebody who makes you feel like an equal
half.
The kind of guy who shows you affection,
One who offers you emotional protection.

Find a guy who is smart with money,
Somebody who makes your day feel a little
more sunny.
A guy who is fun and spontaneous,
The kind of guy who pays attention when you're
out of his radius.

Find a guy that misses you when you're apart,
A guy that makes it known you have his heart.
A guy who knows how to be patient,
Somebody who won't settle and become
complacent.

Find a guy with whom you have great chemistry,
Bonus points if he has a lemon tree.
A guy who appreciates your art,

And encourages you when you need a push start.

Find a guy that respects you as a mother,
And wants to co-parent, even though the father
is someone other.
A guy who sits beside you as you heal your
heartache,
A guy who will hold you when you just need a
break.

Find a guy that shows that your truest form, you
no longer have to hide,
A guy who really enjoys smacking your
backside.
Finally, find a guy that makes your heart glow,
And then enjoy watching the pair of you grow.

Self-Love.

Loving my body is a daily task,
Retraining my mind after a life of self-hate.
After so many years it's hard to take off that
mask,
To learn to love myself at my current weight.

Re-framing my mind to appreciate the skin I'm
in,
For my body nurtured three healthy humans.
Learning to love my body when she is thick or
thin,
Slowly easing my self-image delusions.

I now embrace my squishy tum,
And love my body when I'm nude.
I admire my nice round bum,
Changing my mindset has also changed my
mood.

Hating my body exudes so much energy,
When it's much kinder to love my curves.

Creating happy memories,
Which at the end of the day is truly what my
body deserves.

Heavy Nights.

The nights are heavy, as my mind runs wild,
Inundated with worries about each child.
Fears about my current life,
How much longer will I be his wife?

The nights are heavy as panic consumes me,
Feeling so trapped, just wanting to be free.
Will I ever escape or is this my chosen fate?
Finding it hard to be able to think straight.

The nights are heavy as I lay silently and weep,
While the world around me continues to sleep.
Doubt consumes me, feeling like ill never really
be happy,
Worried ill walk around forever feeling super
crappy.

The nights are heavy as my tears slowly begin to
subside,
I remind myself that at least today I actually
tried.

But now I'm exhausted and should try to get
some rest,
For tomorrow I can start again and try my best.

Pen to paper.

Pen to paper, to clear my mind.,
Releasing the overwhelming feeling from
within.
Taking this fleeting moment,
Before my motherhood duties resume.

I sit and I scribble, pages of notes,
Feeling my emotions release.
Letting my guard down, for just a moment,
Admitting to myself how difficult my life these
days can be.

A temporary pause, in an otherwise chaotic life,
A moment to myself for vulnerability.
To feel relief, wash over me
Pen to paper, to let myself just be me.

PND & Me.

The days blur, as you lose the concept of time,
You watch the sunrise & you watch the sunset.
You feel like a zombie,
Like you're on constant auto pilot.

As time goes on, you regain control,
You feel like yourself.
Kind of, but not really,
You're tired, always tired.

Your body is yours, most of the time,
But it feels different.
Plumper, lumpier, it sags more now,
You're tired, always tired.

Your emotions feel out of control,
You're happy, excited, hopeful.
But then you're sad, anxious, unhappy,
You're never alone, but always feel lonely.

You're so in love,

But you feel like you've lost yourself.
You feel guilty for feeling like this,
You're having a hard time, which you're scared
to admit.

But when you do, and eventually you do,
You feel relief wash over you.
Because you're not alone,
There are so many others feeling this way too.

Our Autistic World.

When my child received a diagnosis of ASD,
The whole world changed for me.
I worried about his future every day,
Would he ever learn how to play?

Would he ever learn to talk,
Or will people forever stare and gawk?
Will he learn to toilet train,
And learn to keep his clothes on, in the rain?

Will he ever look others in the eye,
Would he ever want to hug other people
goodbye?
Can he build a relationship with a significant
other,
Or will he always live with me, his mother?

For four years now we have lived in the autism
world,
We have soldiered through many obstacles that
have been hurled.
He now happily leaves the house,

And is no longer quiet like a little mouse.

He tells me he loves me every single day,
And enjoys the company of others when he
wants to play.
He keeps all his toys in neat rows,
And still walks on his tippy toes.

But he's grown so much and fills my heart with
so much pride,
I know our futures will be a fun and adventurous
ride.
My baby boy he will always be,
And I'll always be there for him, watching him
be free.

The ADHD Loop.

Life is busy and sometimes it's rough,
Often it feels a little too tough.

Sit still, now move around,
Stand up, okay it's time to sit on the ground.

Talk more, but not that much,
Look, but be sure not to touch.

Interests repeatedly on a loop,
Trying to jump through academia hoops.

Inattention and struggling to focus,
Feeling as though someone may try to poke us.

Forget what we're meant to be doing
immediately,
Expecting us to listen obediently.

Despite the struggles,
Our world is full of chuckles.

19

Fidgeting, flapping, jumping, spinning,
Our happy little boy doesn't stop grinning.

Self-Growth.

I am doing this on my own,
Raising the children, until they are grown.
Single parenting was something I didn't think I
could do,
But I knew it was something I had to pursue.

Fear of failure,
Fear of their behaviour.
Fear of heartache,
Fear of making another mistake.

Searching within myself, high and low,
Allowing self-love to grow.
My heart slowly began to heal,
Finally able to feel.

Tears, self-doubt, worries all fell by the wayside.
Recovering from the all the tears I cried.
Stronger, healthier, happier everyday,
Loving my life now in every possible way.

When depression takes over.

21

My brain lies to me often,
Always telling me to proceed with caution.
It fills me with self-doubt and fear,
That things are never as they appear.

It sends me into a deep depression,
All the progress I've made seems to go into a
regression.
Sadness floods through my veins,
It feels nearly impossible to take the reins.

Darkness completely engulfs me,
And it can be so hard to break free.
I feel like I'm drowning,
My heart just won't stop pounding.

I seem to hit my lowest of low,
Then there is nowhere else left to go.
Medication helps by making my body numb,
I often feel like I'm stuck under its thumb.

Eventually the dark clouds begin to clear,
The negative thoughts I no longer hear.
The days start to feel sunny,
I'm able to laugh at things that are funny.

The depressive episode has ended for now,
The negative thoughts have allowed me to smile
somehow.
Finally, leaving this negative space,
Moving and healing at my own pace.

There was love, once.

It wasn't sudden, it was slow, gradual,
I didn't even realize it was happening.
First the romance died down,
Date nights were scarce, and intimacy faded.

Sex was quick and matter of fact,
We didn't devote time to one another.
We made excuses for not spending time
together,
Believing it will be easier when the kids are
older.

We began to prioritize different things,
Both heading in two different directions.
Sitting together in the same room,
Although our worlds couldn't be further apart.

Communication was at an all-time low,
So willing to avoid the real issues.
There was no fighting, no laughter either,
We became the perfect housemates.

My days felt monotonous,
depression at an all-time high.
His shut-down technique perfected,
Finding it easier to distract himself from the
issues at bay.

As the end approached, we were no longer in
love,
We became strangers to one another.
There was love, once,
But it was lost, somewhere along the way.

No apology and that's okay.

You never said you're sorry,
For what you did to me.
Now I know ill never get an apology,
For you choosing the most hurtful way to be
free.

You made so many excuses,
To avoid responsibility.
Alas, your credibility reduces,
And encourages my thoughts of infidelity.

I'm hurt and angry for how I was treated,
Made to feel like I was mentally unstable.
For so long I was left feeling defeated,
Where in reality I was more than able.

I was alone and isolated,
When you dropped your bomb on me.
My heart felt like it disintegrated
After I calmed myself, I knew I had to agree.

For the love we once had, died long ago,
I knew I didn't want to stay but I was scared to
start anew.
But, it was time for me to allow myself to grow,
I became a single mum, and decided, to my own
heart I had to be true.

Over 2 years have passed since I started my new
life,
I never received my sorry and for me, that is
okay,
I'm so much happier not being his wife.
And I'm proud of myself everyday, for having
the courage not to stay.

Walking away.

Walk away when you don't feel valued,
When you feel your needs have fallen by the
wayside.
Walk away when you don't feel like an equal,
When you speak but aren't heard.

Walk away when you're not made a priority,
When you're lied to every day.
Walk away when disappointment is all you feel,
When happy days are few & far between.

Know your worth,
Know your value,
You deserve happiness,
You deserve love.

Walk away because disappointment hurts,
Walk away because you deserve the truth,
Walk away because you should always feel
equal,
Walk away because you are worth so much
more.

The Last Time.

A single tear runs down your face,
As you sit frozen in place.
Your body is still, but you know who we are,
You're taken in ambulance; we follow by car.

Our worry intensifies as we drive,
Praying constantly that you will survive.
At the hospital they tell us you have had an
irreversible stroke,
In that moment, you could hear as my heart
broke.

The whole family is there, to say our last
goodbyes,
Tears silently falling from our eyes.
We hold your hand for the last time, wishing this
was a mistake,
Hoping somehow you would just wake.

We feel surrounded by death,
As you take your last breath.
Our hearts leave the hospital broken,

All the words we never got to share, left unspoken.

Thirty

Turning thirty is a celebration,
In many ways it feels like liberation.
Saying goodbye to the last decade,
While reminiscing on the memories made.

As the day approaches, there's been deep
reflection,
Deciding to move in a new direction.
Developing a new prerogative,
To live life being positive.

Making a conscious choice to focus on feeling
free,
And letting things out of my control, just be.
Being grateful for every day on this earth,
And spending time realizing my worth.

Turning thirty and no longer feeling
apprehension,
Letting my body release the tension.
Looking forward to starting the next year,
Allowing myself to be truly sincere.

Her reasons to smile.

31

She smiles because of the rain.

She smiles because she is no longer in pain.

She smiles because of sunny days.

She smiles because of her children she gets to raise.

She smiles because her heart feels whole.

She smiles because she has regained control.

She smiles because the flowers are in bloom.

She smiles because she no longer feels a sense of doom.

She smiles because of the calm blue sea.

She smiles because she is finally free.